THE ULTIMATE BAKING BIBLE

Easy/Simple Baking Handbook

Mitchell Patrick

All rights reserved. No part of the may be reproduces, distributed or transmitted in any form or by any means, including photocopying, recording, or other electronic or mechanical methods, without the prior written permission of the publisher, except in the case of brief questions embodied in critical reviews and certain other noncommercial uses permitted by copyright law.

Copyright © Mitchell Patrick, 2023.

Table of Content

Outrageous Brownies
Easy Peasy Lemon and Almond Drizzle Loaves
Rocky Road
Victoria Sponge Cake
Caramel Chocolate Shortcake
Lemon Pound Cake
S'mores Cookie Crumble Bars
Chocolate Amaretti Cake
One Bowl Cocoa Brownies
Freezer to Oven Berry Muffins
Red, White and Blueberry Trifle
Egg-Free Banana Passion Fruit Cupcakes
Chocolate Peanut Butter and Banana Icebox Cake
Lemon Icebox Rounds
Banana Walnut Bread
Chocolate Vanilla Sandwich Biscuits
Vanilla Cheesecake
Chocolate Brownies
Lemon Drizzle Cake
Twiggy's Coconut Cake
Chocolate Beetroot Cake
No Butter Ginger Cake
Ham and Cheese Quick Bread
Chocolate Truffle Fudge Cake
Cheese Soda Bread
Angel Food Cake

Bird's Nests
Chocolate Slice Cookies
Vanilla Bean Spritz Shortbread
Marbled Banana Bread
Strawberries and Cream Sponge Cake
Olive Oil Muffins
Easy Banana Muffins
Caramel Cake
.Strawberry Shortcut Cake
Coconut-lime pudding cake
Yummy Brownie Muffins
Sour Cream Pecan Coffee Cake
Carrot Muffins
Chocolate Sables
Easy Apple Fritter Doughnuts

Outrageous Brownies

Ingredients

- 175g of white flour
- 1-tablespoon baking powder
- 360g of chopped walnuts, 1 teaspoon salt
- Sugar, caster, 315 g
- 2 tablespoons pure vanilla extract

- Milk chocolate chips, 790g
- 170g chocolate powder without sugar
- 6 big eggs.
- Granulated instant coffee, 3 tablespoons
- Unsalted butter, 450g

Method

1) Set the oven to 180°C or the gas mark. 4. Grease and flour a baking sheet measuring 30 by 46 by 2 cm.

2) In a medium dish set over simmering water, melt the butter, 450g of chocolate chips, and unsweetened chocolate. Allow to gently cool.

3) Stir the eggs, coffee granules, vanilla, and sugar in a large bowl—do not beat. After allowing it to cool to room temperature, stir the warm chocolate mixture into the egg mixture.

4) Combine 140g of flour, salt, and baking powder in a larger basin. Include in the cooled chocolate amalgamation. In a medium bowl, combine 35g of flour with the walnuts and 340g of chocolate chips. Add this mixture to the chocolate batter.

5) Transfer the batter to the baking dish. After 20 minutes of baking, knock the baking sheet against an oven shelf to compel air to escape from the space between the pan and the brownie batter.

6) Continue baking for an additional 15 minutes, or until a cocktail stick is clean. Avoid overbaking! Allow it completely cool, then cut it into 20 large squares in the refrigerator.

Easy Peasy Lemon and Almond Drizzle Loaves

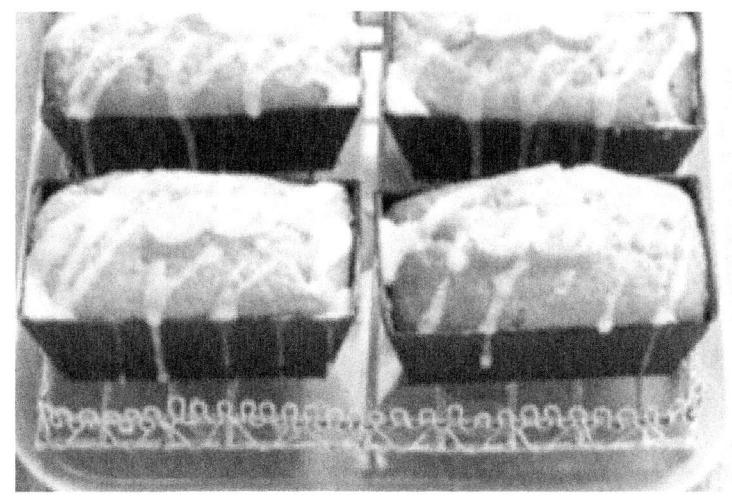

Ingredients

For the syrup
- two lemons juice
- 20 sugared lemon decorations

- 250g fondant icing sugar, sieved

- 50g of almond meal
- 250 grams of golden caster sugar and 200 grams of self-rising flour
- 4 big eggs
- Zest of 2 lemons
- Juice of 1 lemon
- 250g block of margarine

Method

1) Set the oven to Gas or 180°C. Mark 4. The 10 paper loaf pans should be placed on a metal tray.

2) To make the margarine and sugar frothy and light, cream them together. Add the eggs, lemon juice, and zest gradually.

3) Combine the flour and almonds by evenly folding them in.

4) Pour the mixture into the loaf pans made of paper. Bake for 20 minutes, or until golden brown and well-risen.

5) Combine 100g of fondant icing sugar and 1 lemon juice.

6) Place a cooling rack underneath the cakes. With a stick, pierce the cakes numerous times. To cover the cakes, pour the lemon syrup over them.

7) Blend the remaining fondant icing sugar with the lemon juice. Add lemon sugar embellishments to cakes and sprinkle over lemon icing. For up to two days, store in an airtight container.

Rocky Road

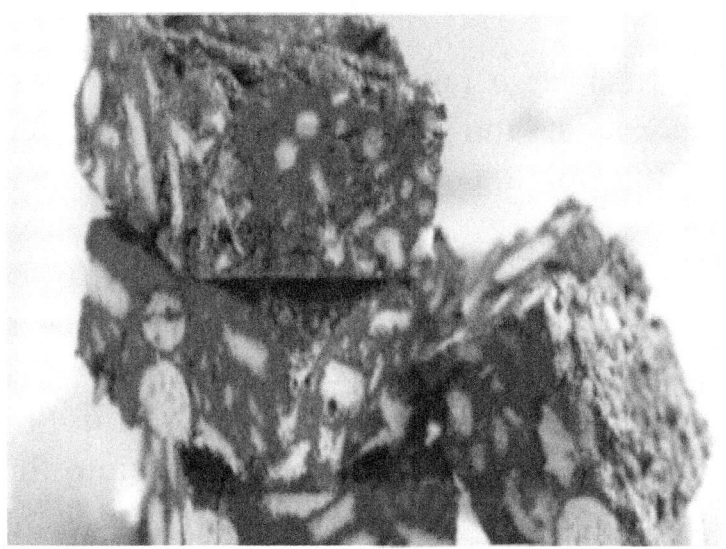

Ingredients
- 12 pink marshmallows, quartered using scissors
- 2 x 55g of Maltesers (my favorite), Milky Way or Crunchie
- 140g rich tea biscuits, roughly crushed
- 3 tbsp golden syrup

- 300g dark chocolate, broken into squares
- 100g butter, roughly chopped

Method

1) In a large pan, slowly melt the butter, chocolate, and syrup while stirring often until smooth. Let cool for about 15 minutes.

2) Pour the mixture into a 17cm (6 12 inches) square baking pan that has been prepared with non-stick baking paper and spread the mixture to roughly level it. Stir the crumbled cookies and candies into the pan until well combined.

3) Chill until solid, then remove from tin and peel off paper. Slice the fingers. In an airtight container, store.

Victoria Sponge Cake

Ingredients
For the filling
- 225g (8 oz) icing sugar, sieved
- For the vanilla icing
- 85g (3 oz) Stork tub
- 1-2 tablespoon milk
- 1/2 teaspoon vanilla essence
- 3 tablespoons jam

For the cake
- 225g (8 oz) caster sugar
- 225g (8 oz) Stork tub
- 4 medium eggs
- 225g (8 oz) self-raising flour, sieved
- 1 level teaspoon baking powder
-

Method

1) Set your oven to Gas 4 at 170°C, 160°C fan.

2) Combine all the ingredients for the sponge in a basin and stir with a wooden spoon for 2 to 3 minutes, or until the mixture is smooth and well combined.

3) Divide your batter between two 20 cm (8 in) sandwich pans that have been greased and lined on the bottom.

4) Place them in the center of the preheated oven and bake for 30-35 minutes, or until they are gorgeously golden.

5) Remove the paper, turn them out, and let them cool on a cake rack.

6) Place the two pieces together, spread the jam in the center, and top with icing sugar.

7) Alternatively, for something even more delectable, combine the ingredients for the vanilla icing in a bowl and whisk until well combined. Spread the mixture over the cake's top and middle.

Caramel Chocolate Shortcake

Ingredients
- 2 tbsp Lyle's Golden Syrup®
- 150ml condensed milk

For the topping
- 150g dark chocolate
- 50g Tate & Lyle® Caster Sugar
- 125g butter
- 125g butter

- 50g caster sugar
- 175g plain flour, sieved

Method

1) Set the oven's temperature to 180°C/350°F/Gas mark 4. For the base, cream together the butter and sugar until light and fluffy. When the ingredients are well combined, add the flour and whisk. Until it's smooth, kneads.

2) Evenly press this dough onto a 20 cm square baking pan, then prick the top with a fork. Remove from the oven after 25 to 30 minutes and let cool in the tin.

3) In the meantime, combine the filling ingredients in a skillet and heat while stirring until the sugar dissolves. Slowly bring to a boil, then simmer for 5-7 minutes while stirring constantly. Pour over the biscuit after a little cooling period to solidify.

4) To prepare the topping, melt the dark chocolate in a glass bowl set over a pot of simmering water. Then, distribute the melted chocolate over the caramel. Keep in the refrigerator until set.

Lemon Pound Cake

Ingredients

For the glaze
- 1/2 tsp salt
- 3 tbsp fresh lemon juice
- 2 tbsp water
- 85g sugar

- 50g flour
- 120g plain flour
- 1 tbsp finely-grated lemon zest
- 300g sugar
- 5 large eggs, almost at room temperature
- 80g sour cream (full-fat)
- 1 1/2 tsp vanilla extract
- 220g unsalted butter, just cooler than room temperature

Method

1) Grease a 9 x 5-inch loaf pan and preheat the oven to 160°C.

2) Using electric beaters or a mixer with a paddle attachment, beat the butter, sugar, and lemon zest for three minutes at medium speed, until they are light and fluffy. Eggs should be lightly whisked with a fork in a separate bowl before being gradually added to the batter, with each addition being followed by a scraping of the bowl. Sour

cream and vanilla should be combined, then beaten into the batter.

3) Sift the salt, plain flour, and cake flour in a separate bowl; add the dry ingredients to the wet ingredients; stir until well combined, scraping the sides of the bowl as necessary. The batter should be scraped into the prepared pan and tapped a few times to level it and let any air bubbles escape.

When a tester is inserted in the center of the cake, it should come out clean after 65 to 70 minutes of baking. While the cake is still warm from the oven, remove it from the oven and make the glaze.

4) To make the glaze, in a small saucepan over medium heat, combine the sugar, water, and lemon juice. Make holes in the warm pound cake with a bamboo skewer, then coat it with the hot glaze. Before removing the cake to serve, let it cool completely in the pan (the glaze will solidify once the cake is cool).

5) The cake can stay out of the fridge for up to three days if it is well-wrapped.

S'mores Cookie Crumble Bars

Ingredients

- 1/2 teaspoon vanilla extract
- One 4.4-ounce bar milk chocolate, such as Hershey's, broken into pieces
- 1 cup marshmallow creme
- 1 large egg, at room temperature

- 1 1/2 sticks (6 ounces) unsalted butter, softened
- 1 1/2 cups all-purpose flour
- 2/3 cup icing sugar
- 1/2 teaspoon salt
- 8 sheets digestive biscuits, finely ground, or 1 cup store-bought graham cracker crumbs

Method

1) Set the oven's temperature to 350 F. Aluminum foil should be used to line an 8-inch square baking dish, providing a 2-inch overhang on each edge of the pan for pulling out the final bars.

2) In a small bowl, combine the flour, sugar, salt, and ground Grahams. You are not attempting to include a lot of air into the mixture; instead, you are just creaming the butter, egg, and vanilla in a medium bowl with an electric mixer on low speed until smooth and blended. Add the graham

mixture and beat on low speed until it is barely mixed and forms big crumbles.

3) Distribute around two-thirds of the mixture in the pan and pack it down firmly. The remainder of the chocolate should be distributed evenly over the base, with a few pieces (approximately 1/2 ounce) set aside for garnish. Stretching the crème to cover more of the base, drop spoonfuls of the marshmallow creme over the chocolate. Over the chocolate and creme, scatter the remaining cookie dough in tiny clusters so that the creme is mostly covered.

4) Bake for about 40 minutes, or until the dough is golden brown and the cookie in the center of the pan feels firm. The marshmallow cream will color and puff through the crumble before deflating as it cools. For at least 15 minutes, let the pan cool.

5) To remove the crumble bars from the pan, use the foil overhang. The chocolate chunks that were set aside should be smoothed out in the microwave in 30-second intervals before being drizzled over the cookies. sixteen 2-by-2-inch squares should be cut out. At room temperature or heated, serve.

Note from the Chef: Working with marshmallow creme can be messy. To make it a little bit simpler to handle, lightly cover your measuring cup, spatula, and spoon with vegetable oil or nonstick cooking spray.

Chocolate Amaretti Cake

Ingredients

- 2 tsp grated orange peel
- 4 large eggs
- Unsweetened cocoa powder, for sifting
- 130g sugar
- 120g unsalted butter, room temperature
- 110g dark chocolate

- 150g flaked almonds
- 60 g baby amaretti cookies
- Butter-flavored non-stick cooking spray

Method

1) Set the oven's temperature to 175°C.

2) Use non-stick spray to coat a 23-cm springform pan. Refrigerate. For about a minute, microwave the chocolate, stirring after every 20 seconds, until it is melted and smooth.

3) Put the cookies and almonds in a food processor. Pulse the cookies and almonds until they are thoroughly ground. To a medium bowl, add the nut mixture. Butter and sugar should be added to a food processor and blended until smooth and creamy. Orange peel gratings are added; pulse

One Bowl Cocoa Brownies

Ingredients

- 1 teaspoon fine salt
- 1/2 teaspoon baking powder
- 340g milk chocolate chips
- Suggested topping combinations: white chocolate chips and toasted
- chopped walnuts; cashews and dried cranberries; chopped pretzels and raisins; toasted coconut and chopped

dried pineapple; or any combination of chopped dried fruit, toasted nuts, mini mars
- 60g unsweetened cocoa powder
- 120g plain flour
- 300g sugar
- 230g unsalted butter, melted and cooled
- 1 teaspoon vanilla extract
- 3 large eggs Nonstick cooking spray, for spraying the foil

Method

1) Set the oven's temperature to 175°C. Spray nonstick cooking spray on aluminum foil and line a 9 by 13 inches baking pan.

2) In a larger bowl, combine the sugar, butter, vanilla, and eggs. Mix just till mixed after adding the flour, baking powder, salt, and cocoa powder all at once. Spread the mixture in the prepared tin after stirring in half of the chocolate chips.

3) Bake the brownies for 30 to 35 minutes, or until they start to pull away from the pan's edge and set in the middle. Sprinkle the remaining semisweet chocolate chips right away, then wait for about five minutes to allow the chips to melt. Using a spatula, evenly distribute the melted chips over the top of the brownies. After letting the chocolate cool for about 10 minutes, sprinkle it with the toppings of your choice and gently press them into the chocolate to help them stick. Utilizing the foil, remove the brownies from the pan and allow them to cool completely on a rack. Serve after cutting into 16 squares.

Freezer to Oven Berry Muffins

Ingredients

For the muffins
- 1/2 teaspoon pure vanilla extract
- 1 stick (4 ounces) unsalted butter, melted

For the Topping
- 1/2 cup all-purpose flour

- 4 tablespoons unsalted butter, softened
- 1/2 cup light brown sugar
- 1 cup milk
- 2 large eggs
- 1 3/4 cups all-purpose flour
- 3/4 cup fresh blueberries, raspberries or diced strawberries
- 2/3 cup granulated sugar
- 2 teaspoons baking powder
- 1/2 teaspoon fine salt

Method

For the muffins

1) Use foil muffin cup liners to line a 12-cup muffin pan.

2) In a small bowl, combine the berries with 2 tablespoons of flour. In a big bowl, combine the remaining flour, salt, baking soda, and granulated sugar. In a medium bowl, whisk the milk, melted butter, and

vanilla after beating the eggs until foamy. The wet components should be added after creating a well in the dry ones. Use a rubber spatula to quickly mix the batter.

For the topping

1) In a larger bowl, mix the flour and brown sugar. To create big and medium crumbs, combine the butter with a fork or your fingertips.

2) Scoop just a little bit more than three-quarters of the batter into each muffin cup. Among the cups, distribute the blueberries. With a delicate touch, distribute the topping among the muffins. For about three hours, freeze until set. At this point, the muffins can be transferred to zippered freezer bags and kept for up to two months.

3) Set the oven to 325 degrees Fahrenheit when you are ready to bake. Bake the

muffins for 35 to 40 minutes, or until a tester inserted in the center comes out clean, depending on whether you use a muffin pan or a baking sheet.

4) You can also bake these muffins right away. Bake for 20 to 25 minutes, until the top is lightly brown and a tester inserted in the center comes out clean. Preheat the oven to 350 degrees F.

Red, White and Blueberry Trifle

Ingredients

- 1/2 teaspoon pure vanilla extract
- 480g double cream
- 1 ready-made angel food cake
- Icing sugar, for garnish, optional
- 1 1/2 tablespoons apple jam or apricot preserve, for garnish, optional

- 225g cream cheese
- Pinch salt
- One 170g punnet blackberries
- Two 170g punnets blueberries
- 150g granulated sugar
- 1/2 teaspoon finely grated lemon zest
- 2 tablespoons fresh lemon juice
- Two 450g punnets strawberries

Method

1) Quarter the strawberries, then set them aside. The blueberries, blackberries, 80 ml water, 100 g granulated sugar, lemon zest, juice, and salt are all combined in a medium pot. Over medium heat, bring to a simmer while stirring regularly. Cook for 15 to 20 minutes, stirring occasionally, or until the berries are broken down and the sauce is thick.
After being taken out of the heat, cool.

2) Mix the cream cheese, 60 ml of the cream, the remaining granulated sugar, and

the vanilla extract in a sizable bowl. Whisk until foamy and creamy at medium speed. In a second large bowl, whisk the remaining cream until stiff peaks form. Before adding the remaining whipped cream, the cream cheese mixture should be softened by folding in about a fourth of it.

3) Before putting the trifle together, rip or cut the angel food cake into 2-inch pieces. A trifle dish or a big bowl that accommodates 12 to 14 cups should have the bottom filled with half of the cake pieces. On top, scatter about half of the strawberry quarters, half of the cream, and half of the blueberry sauce. Repeat the layers with the remaining cake, berry sauce, cream, and strawberries. Refrigerate for eight hours or overnight after wrapping with cling film. Either sprinkle confectioners sugar over the strawberries before serving or warm the apple jelly for 25 seconds in the microwave before brushing it on.

Egg-Free Banana Passion Fruit Cupcakes

Ingredients

For the Icing
- 350g icing sugar
- 50g softened butter

For the cake
- 3 passion fruits
- 1 mashed banana
- 2 tsp vanilla extract
- 140g caster sugar
- 2 tsp baking powder
- 40g softened butter
- 120ml milk
- 120g plain flour

Method

1) In a mixing bowl, combine the dry butter (we'll refer to it as "dry" for our purposes), flour, sugar, baking powder, and salt. Mix the ingredients until they resemble fine sand.

2) Fill a jug with milk and vanilla essence, then whisk vigorously. As you pour the liquid and mix the flour, keep doing so until you have a smooth batter or mixture. After

incorporating the mashed banana, give the mixer a little rest and clean the blade.

3) Fill 12 muffin liners evenly, and bake for 20 minutes at 170°C, or until the center spring is back when touched.

4) Prepare the icing by mixing the butter, cream cheese, and icing sugar until it is very light and fluffy while the cake cools on a wire rack.

5) Take two passion fruits and remove the seeds. Add the seeds to your icing. This should be carefully mixed with a spoon until it is fairly even. If you use the mixer now, the passion fruit's seeds will be broken up.

6) Using a reusable piping bag and a large star nozzle, decorate the cakes with icing and a few remaining passion fruit seeds. then offer. Your egg-free friends will be waiting in line to chow down on your treats!

Chocolate Peanut Butter and Banana Icebox Cake

Ingredients
- 1 1/2 teaspoons vanilla extract
- 2 packs of chocolate wafer biscuits
- 5 bananas, sliced, plus additional for garnish
- 120g sugar
- 750ml cold whipping cream

- 130g smooth peanut butter

Method

1) Combine the peanut butter and 1/2 cup heavy cream in a large bowl and whisk with a handheld mixer until smooth. To produce slightly firm peaks, whisk the remaining 2 cups of cream with the sugar and vanilla after making sure the whipping attachments are clean. To lighten the peanut butter mixture, gently fold in some whipped cream. Returning the peanut butter mixture to the whipped cream in three portions, fold it gently to integrate while attempting to maintain its light and airy texture, and then set it aside.

2) Arrange a layer of cookies (approximately 16) in a circle, covering the entire surface of a 9-inch springform pan. Slices of banana should be placed on top of the whipped cream layer that has been spread over the cookies. Repeat the process with the

remaining cookies, whipped cream, and banana slices to create a total of 5 layers. Add a layer of whipped cream on top to complete the dessert. Refrigerate for at least four hours and up to overnight with a plastic wrap covering.

Cook's Note: To assist level out the peanut butter whipped cream in the springform pan, use a baby offset spatula.

Lemon Icebox Rounds

Ingredients
- 1/4 tsp salt
- 2 tsp finely grated lemon zest
- 90g demerara sugar or yellow sugar
- 310g flour, sifted
- 1/2 tsp vanilla extract
- 55g, plus 2 tbsp icing sugar, sifted
- 1 hard boiled egg's yolk

- 1 large egg yolk
- 55g, plus 2 tbsp unsalted butter, room temperature

Method

1) Blend the butter and powdered sugar.

2) Stir the raw egg yolk, lemon, and vanilla into the hard-boiled egg yolk after pressing it through a sieve. This should be mixed in with the butter mixture after being added.

3) Blend the butter mixture by adding the flour and salt and stirring. The dough should be formed into inch-wide logs, which you should then wrap in plastic. For roughly two hours, chill until hard.

4) Set the oven to 180 degrees Celsius and line two baking sheets with parchment paper.

5) Place a dish with the demerara sugar on it. The cookie logs should be unwrapped and then rolled in sugar to coat. Place the

cookies on the baking sheets, cutting them into slices about 1/4 inch thick and spacing them out by 1/2 inch. The cookies should be lightly browned on the bottom after baking for about 15 minutes. After the cookies have cooled on the tray, keep them in an airtight container.

If you store the cookies in an airtight container, they can last up to 4 days.

Banana Walnut Bread

Ingredients

- 200g caster sugar
- 3 very ripe bananas, peeled, and mashed with a fork
- 50g toasted walnut pieces, roughly chopped

- 1/2 cup unsalted butter, at room temperature, plus more for preparing the tin
- 1/2 teaspoon vanilla extract
- 1 teaspoon bicarbonate of soda
- 1/2 teaspoon table salt
- 2 large eggs, at room temperature
- 150g plain flour

Method

1) In a medium bowl, sift the salt, bicarbonate of soda, and flour. In a liquid measuring cup with a spout, combine the eggs and vanilla; leave aside. Lightly butter a loaf pan that measures 9 by 5 by 3 inches. the oven to 175 degrees Celsius.

2) Cream the butter and sugar until light and fluffy using an electric hand-held mixer or a stand mixer with a paddle attachment. Pour the egg mixture into the butter in small batches and stir until combined. Remove the bowl from the mixer after adding the

bananas (the mixture will look to be curdled, but don't panic).

3) Add the flour mixture and stir with a rubber spatula until just combined. After adding the nuts, pour the batter into the pan that has been prepared. A toothpick put into the center of the bread should come out clean after 55 minutes of baking. For five minutes, let the bread cool on a wire rack inside the pan. The bread should be removed from the pan and allowed to cool entirely on a rack. Cling film it up. The banana bread tastes the finest the next day.

Chocolate Vanilla Sandwich Biscuits

Ingredients

- 1/4 tsp baking powder
- 1/4 tsp salt
- 6oz fondant icing
- 1/4 cup cocoa powder
- 1 1/4 cups plain flour

- 1/2 cup sugar
- 1 large egg yolk
- 1 tsp vanilla extract
- 1/2 cup + 2 tbsp unsalted butter at room temperature

Method

1) Combine butter and sugar and beat till frothy. After adding the vanilla, whisk in the egg yolk.

2) Sift the flour, cocoa powder, baking powder, and salt into another bowl. This should be mixed in with the butter after being added. Divide into 2 discs, wrap, and chill for at least one hour or until hard.

2) Prepare two baking trays with parchment paper and preheat the oven to 175°C. To prevent the dough from cracking when rolling, give it one or two kneads on a surface dusted with flour. Then, roll the dough out to a thickness of just less than 1/4

inch. Use a 2-inch cookie cutter to cut out cookies, then transfer them to baking trays. If the dough becomes too soft when rolling, simply refrigerate it for 15 minutes before rolling again. Any leftover scraps can also be reused.

4) Bake the biscuits for 8 minutes or until they start to lose their shine. Before removing the biscuits to fill, let them cool on the tray.

5) Using the same cookie cutter as for the biscuits, cut 2-inch circles out of the fondant by rolling it out to a thickness of slightly over 1/8 inch using icing sugar rather than flour. Apply a little water to one side of the fondant and press it to the bottom of one cookie. Put the bottom of a second biscuit on top of the fondant, brush the opposite side with a little water, and press lightly to seal the sandwich. Reroll the fondant if necessary and repeat with the remaining biscuits.

6) You can keep the biscuits for up to three days in an airtight container.

.

Vanilla Cheesecake

Ingredients

- 1 lemon, zested
- 160g caster sugar
- 160ml sour cream
- 160ml double cream
- Splash of vanilla extract
- 475g cream cheese
- 1 dsp caster sugar

- 140g digestive biscuits
- Fruit to finish
- Strong coffee or espresso
- 85g butter

Method

1) Melt the butter and sugar in a small saucepan over low heat, then pour the mixture over the crumbled biscuits in a bowl. Completely combine.

2) Greaseproof paper should be used to line a 23 cm springform cake pan. Press the biscuit mixture into the bottom of the baking pan to create a solid, tightly packed base. Allow sitting in the refrigerator for about 30 minutes.

3) Prepare the filler in the interim. To soften the cream cheese, beat it in a bowl with the lemon zest and half the sugar. The sour cream, double cream, remaining sugar, and vanilla extract should all be combined in a

separate dish. Whisk this mixture until it forms firm peaks and is stable enough to be turned over your head.

4) After incorporating the cream into the cream cheese mixture, pour the entire mixture over the cold biscuit base. Refrigerate for at least four hours and ideally all night.

5) You could add fruit on top. To enhance their sweetness, we used fresh strawberries combined with a small amount of icing sugar

Chocolate Brownies

Ingredients

For the coffee topping
- 3 tablespoons milk
- 25g (1 oz) Stork packet
- 1 teaspoon coffee extract
- 12 walnut halves to decorate

- 85g (3 oz) plain chocolate

- 225g (8 oz) soft brown sugar
- 1 tablespoon coffee extract
- 2 large eggs
- 85g (3 oz) plain flour, sieved with 25g (1 oz) cocoa and 1/2 teaspoon baking powder
- 115g (4 oz) Stork packet

Method

1) Set the oven's temperature to 180°C, 160°C fan, and Gas mark 4.

2) Combine the cream cheese, sugar, and coffee flavoring; beat until frothy.

3) Beat well after adding each egg one at a time.

4) Using a metal spoon, fold in the flour, cocoa, and baking powder.

5) Spread evenly in a greased 28 x 18cm (11 x 7 inch) Swiss roll pan.

6) Bake for 25 to 30 minutes in the center of the preheated oven. Turn out onto a wire tray to cool.

7) Melt the chocolate in a basin over boiling water to form the topping. Beat till glossy and smooth after adding the milk and Stork.

8) Add the coffee flavoring and stir.

9) Distribute and then cut into squares the brownies.

10) Use walnuts as decorations.

Lemon Drizzle Cake

Ingredients

- Finely grated rind of 2 lemons
- Juice of 2 lemons, strained
- 115g (4 oz) caster sugar
- 2 tablespoons milk
- 3 medium eggs
- 1 teaspoon baking powder
- 175g (6 oz) Stork tub

- 175g (6 oz) caster sugar
- 175g (6 oz) self raising flour

Method

1) In a large mixing bowl, sift the flour and baking powder. Add the remaining ingredients for the cake and stir with a wooden spoon until smooth.

2) Pour the ingredients into a 1 kilogram (2 lb) loaf pan that has been oiled and lined.

3) Bake for 1 hour, or until done, in a preheated oven at 180°C, 350°F, Gas 4.

4) Remove and place on a wire tray.

5) In a saucepan, combine the sugar and lemon juice. Heat just until the sugar is dissolved.

6) Drizzle the syrup on top of the warm cake so that it soaks in.

7) Slice, then warmly serve.

Twiggy's Coconut Cake

Ingredients

- 1 egg
- 125ml milk
- 1 tsp vanilla extract
- 75g butter
- 1/2 tsp lemon zest
- 75g sugar

- 50g desiccated coconut
- 1/2 tsp salt
- 2 tsp baking powder
- 200g plain flour

Method

1) Set the oven's temperature to 180oC/350F/gas mark 4. In a bowl, sift together the flour, salt, and baking powder. Butter should feel like fine breadcrumbs after being rubbed in. Sugar, lemon zest, and coconut are added.

2) In another bowl, whisk the egg and add the milk and vanilla essence. To add the liquid egg/milk combination, make a hole in the flour mixture. Blend everything until the mixture is firm. Whenever more milk is required, add it.

3) Put the mixture in a greased 15cm (6-inch) round cake pan and bake for 40

minutes at 180°C (350°F) or Gas Mark 4 or until a knife inserted in the center comes out clean.

Chocolate Beetroot Cake

Ingredients

- 1 level tsp bicarbonate of soda
- 1 level tsp baking powder
- ½ tsp salt
- ½ tsp vanilla extract
- Damson jam (to fill the cake)

- Grated zest of a large orange
- 200g plain flour
- 1 heaped tsp allspice
- 100g dark muscovado sugar
- 200g soft light brown sugar
- 300ml sunflower oil
- 300g vacuum packed beetroot (without vinegar), drained
- 100g cocoa powder
- 3 large eggs

Method

1) Prepare two 18 cm (7") sandwich pans by greasing them and lining the bases with baking paper.

2) Set the oven's temperature to 190°C (fan 180°C).

3) Mix the eggs, sugars, and oil in a food processor until they are thick and creamy. Take out into a sizable mixing basin.

4) Use a food processor to finely chop the beetroot and purée it.

5) Combine the beetroot with the cocoa powder and spices.

6) Combine with the egg mixture after adding.

7) Add the vanilla essence and orange zest to the bowl after sifting the dry ingredients there. Then, fold everything together thoroughly with a metal spoon.

8) Distribute the batter between the two sandwich pans, and bake for 35 minutes, or until a cocktail stick inserted into the center of the cakes comes out clean. The cake's color will be very dark.

9) Enable cooling on wire racks.

10) When completely cold, sandwich with about 1/2 jar of Damson jam.

No Butter Ginger Cake

Ingredients

- 1 carton drinking chocolate
- 5 balls stem ginger finely chopped (this comes in a jar with syrup)
- A small drizzle of the ginger syrup
- 3 beaten eggs
- 2 cartons self raising flour
- 2 cartons of caster sugar

- 1 carton of sunflower oil
- 175g carton plain yoghurt (the measurements for the rest of the cake are measured using the empty yoghurt carton)

Method

1) A 7-inch round cake pan should be greased and lined.

2) Set oven temperature to 170°C/Gas mark 3.

3) Combine all the ingredients in a basin, then pour the batter into the prepared pan. Bake the cake in the center of the oven for about 1 hour and 45 minutes, or until a skewer inserted in the center comes out clean.

4) After allowing the cake to cool in the pan for about 10 minutes, take it out onto a wire

rack and brush the top with some ginger syrup. Hold back till cool.

Ham and Cheese Quick Bread

Ingredients

- 3 eggs
- 2 tablespoons honey
- 170g deli ham, finely chopped
- 85g gruyere cheese, grated

- 2 spring onions, chopped
- 55g gruyere cheese, diced
- 80ml vegetable oil
- 180ml milk, plus 1 tablespoon
- 1 1/4 teaspoons baking powder
- 240g plain flour
- 3/4 teaspoon bicarbonate of soda
- 2 1/4 teaspoons dry mustard
- Pinch cayenne pepper
- 1/2 teaspoon sea salt
- Non-stick cooking spray

Method

1) Set the oven's temperature to 175°C. Spray a metal loaf pan measuring 9 by 5 by 3 inches with nonstick cooking spray sparingly, then set it aside.

2) Combine the flour, baking powder, bicarbonate of soda, salt, cayenne, and 3/4 teaspoon dry mustard in a medium bowl. 180 ml of milk, the oil, one spoonful of honey, and the eggs should all be thoroughly

combined in a big dish. Add the dry ingredients and mix just enough to blend. After that, incorporate the ham, cheese (reserving some for topping), cheese dice, and spring onions.

3) Place the batter in the loaf pan that has been preheated, and then top with the remaining cheese. Bake for 40 to 45 minutes, or until the top is well-risen, and golden brown, and a skewer or cake tester inserted in the center comes out clean.

4) Let cool for ten minutes in the pan. The remaining 1 tablespoon of both honey and milk, together with the remaining 1 1/2 teaspoons of dried mustard, should be combined well in a small microwave-safe bowl. Heat for 20 to 30 seconds in the microwave until hot and bubbling. Brush the heated glaze liberally all over the loaf before turning it onto a wire rack. Complete cooling.

Chocolate Truffle Fudge Cake

Ingredients

- Nip of rum or whisky
- 75g chocolate cake crumbs
- 60g glace cherries
- 75g raisins
- 250g dark chocolate
- 500g packet of digestives – crushed or blitzed in food processor
- 1 tbsp cocoa

- 55g caster sugar
- 2 tbsp golden syrup
- 2 tbsp milk
- 2 tbsp drinking chocolate
- 250g butter

Method

1) This is delectable and so simple that an oven is not even required. The measurement is where all the labor is. Additionally, the airtight container keeps the food fresh for a good few days.

2) In a big saucepan, melt the butter, sugar, milk, and golden syrup over low heat. Add the cocoa, sipping chocolate, and half of the biscuits when the sugar has dissolved.

3) Combine thoroughly before adding all the additional ingredients—aside from the chocolate. In a 20 cm (8 in) square pan, press the ingredients.

4) While the water in a pan is boiling, melt the dark chocolate. When finished, spread it over the biscuit foundation and allow it to set. 30 tiny bars should result from this. Delicious!

Cheese Soda Bread

Ingredients

- 275ml buttermilk
- 1 large egg, beaten
- 1-2 tbsp semi-skimmed milk
- Flour, for dusting

- Freshly ground black pepper
- 1 tsp salt
- 450g self-raising flour
- 1 tbsp rapeseed oil
- 1 large leek, thinly sliced
- ½ tablespoon dried sage
- 75g mature English Cheddar, grated
- Butter, for greasing

Method

1) Set the oven to 190°C with the fan on. 5 gas mark at 170 °C.

2) Apply butter to a baking sheet. Leeks should be gently cooked for 10 minutes, or until they are just beginning to brown, in oil in a medium nonstick frying pan. Sage should be added after cooling.

3) Combine the leeks, sage, cheese, flour, salt, and some freshly ground black pepper in a large mixing dish. The mixture should

now include the beaten egg. The buttermilk should now be added gradually until the dough is smooth. Perhaps you should add more milk. If the dough is sticky, don't worry. Bring the dough together by transferring it to a work surface that has been dusted with flour. Create a circular out of the dough that is about 23 cm (9 in) in diameter.

4) Place the dough on the prepared baking sheet and flatten it into a circle. Make six wedges by making deep incisions across the top, then bake the bread for 30-35 minutes, or until golden brown. To cool, transfer to a wire rack.

5) Although the bread is best served warm, it can be stored for a few days if not used right once.

Angel Food Cake

Ingredients

- 55g icing sugar, sifted
- 1/2 tsp vanilla extract
- Whipped cream and berries to serve
- 1/8 tsp salt
- 1/2 cream of tartar
- 200g sugar

- 8 large egg whites, room temperature
- 120g flour

Method

1) Set the oven's temperature to 180°C.

2) Double-sift the flour and sugar, then place them in a separate bowl.

3) Whip the egg whites until frothy, adding salt, cream of tartar, and icing sugar as you go. Continue whipping the egg whites until they hold a medium peak when the beaters are raised. Add the vanilla and mix.

4) Add the flour in two portions, folding it in smoothly and evenly with a whisk after each addition. In a 10-inch, oiled tube pan, scrape the mixture into the pan and smooth it out evenly. Bake the cake for 30-35 minutes, or until it springs back when lightly pressed (avoid opening the oven before 25 minutes).

5) To cool the cake, flip the pan over; do not remove the cake from the pan until it has cooled fully. Invert the pan and tap it on the counter until the cake comes out. To remove, carefully run a palette knife along the exterior of the cake and very lightly around the inner tube.

6) If desired, top the cake with whipped cream and berries before serving.

7) The cake keeps for up to 3 days when properly covered but not refrigerated.

Bird's Nests

Ingredients

For the assembly
- 1 tbsp sugar
- 1/2 tsp vanilla extract
- Large handful mixed fresh berries
- 180ml whipping cream

For the nests
- 3 large egg whites, at room temperature
- 3/8 tsp cream of tartar
- 150g sugar

Method

1) Turn the oven on to 150 C. On parchment paper, draw six circles with a marker that are each
2 1/2 inches around and have at least 2 inches between them. Then, flip the paper over onto a baking sheet.

2) Whisk the egg whites and cream of tartar on low speed first, then raise the speed after the whites are frothy and gradually add the sugar as you continue to whisk. Whip the whites continuously until they maintain a firm peak when the beaters are lifted.

3) Fill a piping bag with meringue and fit a large star tip on it. Fill the circles within the

lines on the parchment. To create the "nest" impression, pipe a ring or meringue on top of the outer edge, spiraling up to about 2 inches above the base.

4) Immediately after putting the meringues in the oven, lower the temperature to 135°C. Meringues should be baked for 45 to 65 minutes, depending on the ambient temperature and humidity. If it's hot or humid outside, baking time will increase. Open the oven door and keep baking if you notice that the meringues are turning brown. On the baking sheet, allow the meringues to cool completely to room temperature before gently lifting them to store in an airtight container until ready to serve.

5) Whip the cream to soft peaks before folding in the sugar and vanilla for assembly. Put a bird's nest on each plate, place a dollop of cream in the center, and

then sprinkle berries on top. Serve right away.

6) The meringues can be prepared a day ahead of time, but they need to be put together right before serving.

Chocolate Slice Cookies

Ingredients

- 2 tbsp cornflour
- 1/2 tsp salt
- Icing sugar, for dusting
- 1/4 cup cocoa powder
- 1 cup cake and pastry flour
- 1/2 cup icing sugar, sifted
- 3 large egg yolks

- 1/2 cup unsalted butter, at room temperature

Method

1) After smoothing out the butter and sugar, add the egg yolks all at once and continue beating until thoroughly blended.

2) Sift the flour, cocoa powder, cornstarch, and salt in another bowl. Add this and mix it well with the butter mixture. The dough should be formed into a log with a diameter of about 2 inches, wrapped, and chilled until needed.

3) Set the oven to 325°F and prepare the icebox cookies. Use parchment paper to line 2 baking pans.

4) Arrange the dough pieces, which should be about 1/8-inch thick, on the prepared baking trays. Bake for 12 minutes or until

they lose their shine. Dust the cookies with icing sugar when they have cooled.

5) The cookies can be stored for up to 4 days in an airtight container.

Vanilla Bean Spritz Shortbread

Ingredients

- 1/3 cup cornflour
- ¼ tsp salt
- 1 ½ cups plain flour

- 1 ½ tsp vanilla pod paste
- 1 cup icing sugar, sifted
- 1 ¼ cups unsalted butter at room temperature

Method

1) Provide 40 cookies.

2) Set the oven to 325 degrees Fahrenheit and cover two baking trays with parchment paper.

3) For about 3 minutes, beat the butter and icing sugar until they are light and fluffy. Vanilla bean paste (or extract) should be beaten in. When creating shortbread, it's crucial to thoroughly combine the butter and sugar; doing so ensures that the shortbread will stick together and "snap" when you take a piece before melting.

4) Sift the flour, cornstarch, and salt together in a separate dish, then add to the

softened butter and stir to combine. Spoon the dough into a cookie press or a piping bag with a large star tip. One inch should separate each cookie when you pipe them onto the baking trays that have been prepared.

5) Bake immediately for a spreadable, flatter cookie. The unbaked cookies that have been piped should be chilled for 15 minutes before baking for a cookie that sits up and keeps its shape. Bake the cookies for 20 to 25 minutes, or until the bottoms are just starting to faintly brown. Before putting the cookies in an airtight container, let them cool on the baking sheets.

6) You can store the cookies for up to a week.

Marbled Banana Bread

Ingredients

- 1/2 teaspoon bicarbonate of soda
- 1 1/2 teaspoons baking powder
- 1/2 teaspoon salt

- 1/2 cup buttermilk
- 1 teaspoon vanilla extract
- 3/4 cup white wholemeal flour
- 2 large eggs
- 2 ounces dark chocolate, chopped
- 3/4 cup plain flour, plus extra for dusting the pan
- 2 medium overripe bananas
- 2/3 cup sugar
- 1/4 cup canola oil
- Nonstick cooking spray

Method

1) Set the oven's temperature to 175°C. Use nonstick cooking spray to lightly spritz a metal loaf pan measuring 9 by 5 inches. Then, evenly coat the pan with all-purpose flour, tapping off any excess.

2) Place the chocolate in a medium microwave-safe bowl. Microwave on high for 30-second intervals, stirring after each one, until the chocolate is smooth and

melted, about 1 minute. While making the batter, set it aside to allow it slightly cool.

3) In a large basin, combine the bananas and sugar. Using a potato masher or fork, mash the mixture until mostly smooth and there are only a few tiny chunks of banana left. Stir in the oil and eggs after adding them. Mix in the baking powder, baking soda, salt, and both flours using a wooden spoon or rubber spatula. Add the vanilla and buttermilk and stir.

4) Combine the melted chocolate with 1 cup of the batter. Half of the chocolate batter and then half of the banana batter should be poured into the loaf pan. Use a spoon or knife to gently swirl the layers together after repeating them. Bake for about 45 minutes, or until the top is golden brown and a toothpick inserted in the center comes out clean.

5) Let the pan cool for 15 minutes before transferring it to a wire rack to finish cooling. At room temperature or heated, serve.

Strawberries and Cream Sponge Cake

Ingredients

For the Cream and Berries
- 1/2 teaspoon lemon zest
- 1/3 cup sugar

- 1/2 125g package brick cream cheese, at room temperature
- 2 tablespoons lemon juice
- 1 teaspoon vanilla extract or vanilla pod paste Icing sugar, for dusting
- 1/3 cup good quality strawberry jam
- 1 quart fresh strawberries, hulled and sliced
- 1 1/2 cups whipping cream

For the Sponge Cake
- 1 tablespoon lemon juice
- 1 cup sugar
- 6 large eggs, at room temperature
- 1 teaspoon finely grated lemon zest
- 1 cup plain flour
- 1 teaspoon vanilla extract
- 2 tablespoons unsalted butter, melted
- 1/4 teaspoon salt

Method

Regarding the Sponge Cake

1) Set the oven's temperature to 325 F. Instead of greasing the pan, line the bottom of a 9-inch springform pan with parchment paper.

2) Whip the eggs and sugar at high speed for about 5 minutes, or until they are nearly white, more than triple in volume, and hold a ribbon when the beaters are raised. Add the juice and zest while mixing on medium speed.

3) While the mixer is set to medium speed, sift the flour and salt. Pour about a cup of the batter into a bowl, then add the vanilla and melted butter. Reintroduce everything to the complete batter and whisk to combine. When the center of the cake bounces back when lightly pressed, the

baking time should be around 40 minutes. The cake should cool in the pan.

For the Berries and Cream

1) Whip the cream in a separate bowl until a soft peak forms when the beaters are lifted. Cream cheese should be softened in a separate basin before being combined with sugar, lemon juice, vanilla extract, or vanilla bean paste. Two at a time, fold in the whipped cream. Until you're ready to assemble, chill.

2) Before assembling the cake, combine the berries and jam in a large bowl. To remove the cake from the pan and take off the parchment paper, run a palette knife around the inside edge of the cake pan to loosen it. The cake should be cut in half horizontally. The cake should be covered with half the cream and topped with half the berries. Place the cake's top over the berries, then cover it with the remaining berries and

cream, leaving about an inch or so of the cake's edge exposed. When ready to serve, cover this edge with icing sugar and cool.

3) The cake can be put together up to four hours beforehand.

Olive Oil Muffins

Ingredients

- 2 tbsp whole milk
- 2 tbsp balsamic vinegar
- 190ml extra-virgin olive oil
- 50g sliced almonds, toasted

- Icing sugar, for sifting
- 2 tsp lemon zest
- 2 tsp orange zest
- 2 tsp baking powder
- 1/2 tsp salt
- 200g sugar
- 4 large eggs
- 245g plain flour

Method

1) Turn on the oven's gas or 180°C setting. 4. Fill a 12-cup muffin tray with paper liners.

2) In a larger bowl, thoroughly combine the flour, baking powder, and salt. In a large bowl, combine the sugar, eggs, and zests and beat with an electric mixer until pale and frothy, about three minutes.

3) Combine the milk and vinegar. Beat the oil in slowly. Add the flour mixture and combine briefly after adding. As you add the almonds to the mixture, break them up with your hands and stir until combined.

4) Place paper liners in the muffin tin almost to the top. Bake for 20 to 25 minutes, or until the top is brown and a tester put into the center of the cake comes out with moist crumbs attached.

5) Move the finished product to a wire rack to cool for ten minutes. Place the muffins on a dish and allow them to cool for a further five minutes. Then serve the muffins with icing sugar on top.

Easy Banana Muffins

Ingredients

- 2 large eggs, at room temperature
- 1/8 tsp fine salt
- 1/2 tsp pure vanilla essence
- 75g chopped walnuts
- 125ml milk
- 8 tbsp vegetable oil

- 1/2 tsp bicarbonate of soda
- 130g dark brown sugar
- 1/4 tsp ground cinnamon
- Mashed bananas (about 4 to 6 bananas)
- 350g unbleached plain flour

Method

1) Set the oven's thermostat to 220°C or gas mark 7.

2) Lightly grease a 12-muffin pan and lay it aside.

3) In a larger bowl, combine the cinnamon, brown sugar, bicarbonate of soda, and flour.

4) In a big measuring cup with a spout or another bowl, combine the banana, oil, milk, eggs, salt, and vanilla.

5) In the middle of the dry ingredients, make a tiny well. When the dry ingredients

are moistened but still lumpy, pour the wet components into the center and stir with a wooden spoon. Avoid overmixing the batter to avoid thick muffins. Add the nuts and stir slowly. In the muffin tray, distribute the batter evenly.

6) After placing the muffins in the oven, immediately lower the temperature to the gas mark/190°C. 5. Bake for about 25 minutes, flipping the pan halfway through, until golden brown. (To check if a muffin is done, stick a toothpick into the center. A clean toothpick should be extracted. For a few minutes, let the muffins cool on a rack in the pan. Remove the muffins from the pan, then let them cool on a rack. At room temperature or heated, serve.

Caramel Cake

Ingredients

For the filling
- 115g butter

For the icing

- 1 tsp pure vanilla essence
- 225g packed dark brown sugar
- 80ml double cream, more if needed
- 225g chopped nuts, optional
- 1 tsp pure vanilla essence
- 1 (500g) box icing sugar
- 225g packed light brown sugar
- 60ml milk
- 4 eggs
- 450g caster sugar
- 230g butter, room temperature
- 680g self-rising flour, sifted
- 240ml milk
- 115g butter

For the cake

- 1 tsp pure vanilla essence

Method

1) Set the oven to Gas/180°C. 4. Prepare three (23-cm) cake pans with butter and flour.

2) Whip the butter with an electric mixer until it is light and fluffy. For 6 to 8 minutes after adding the caster sugar, whisk the mixture well again. One at a time beat well after each addition of the eggs. Beginning and ending with the flour, add the milk to the creamed mixture in an alternating fashion. Beat after adding the vanilla until barely combined.

3) Evenly distribute the batter among the prepared pans. Holding the tin 10 cm above the counter and lowering it flat onto the counter will level the batter in each tin. Repeat this multiple times to get rid of any air bubbles and guarantee a leveler cake. 25 minutes in the oven, or until golden brown.

4) Prepare the filling while the cake bakes. Melt the butter, brown sugar, and milk together in a saucepan. For 3 to 5 minutes, mix and cook the food over medium heat. Add the vanilla after turning the heat off.

5) Take the cake layers out of the oven, leaving them in the pans as you get ready to stack and fill them. Invert the cake onto a cake plate after removing the top layer. Use a toothpick to pierce the cake layer all over. On the cake layer, spread a third of the filling mixture. Repeat the procedure for the second and third layers before adding the second layer on top. Cook's tip: To keep the layers from shifting as you stack them, use toothpicks to secure them together.

For the Icing

1) Melt the butter in a saucepan over medium heat, then whisk in the brown sugar and cream to make the caramel icing.

Transfer to a mixing bowl after bringing to a boil.

2) Include the vanilla and icing sugar. Use an electric hand mixer to blend until it has the consistency of spreading. If the frosting becomes too thick at this point, it might be necessary to add another tablespoon or more of double cream. Because you can always add more but not take any away, make sure to add the cream in moderate amounts.

3) Ice the cake and, if wanted, top it with chopped nuts.

.Strawberry Shortcut Cake

Ingredients

- 1 tsp vanilla essence
- 1 (85g) package strawberry flavored jelly mix
- Fresh strawberries, for garnish

- 30g icing sugar
- 240ml double cream
- 500g fresh strawberries, sliced
- 2 tbsp cognac
- 50g caster sugar
- 1 (520g) box strawberry cake mix

Method

1) Set the oven to 180°C or Gas 4.

2) Comply with the cake instructions listed on the cake mix box.

3) Take the cake out of the oven and allow it to cool completely. Strawberries, cognac, and sugar are combined in a medium bowl in the meantime. Macerate for 20 minutes. The cake should be inverted and released onto a pretty dish.

4) Whip cream with vanilla, icing sugar, and a medium-high speed until stiff peaks form. Avoid overwhipping.

5) Prepare the jelly as instructed on the box. Refrigerate the jelly mixture, but do not allow it to get solid; it should cool to a liquid state.

6) Poke holes all over the cake using a straw. Fill up the gaps with jelly before covering the cake's top.

7) Cover the cake's top with a layer of macerated strawberries. On top of the strawberries, add a layer of whipped cream and create attractive ripples and swirls. Use fresh strawberries as a garnish. Place in the fridge for at least 4 hours.

Coconut-lime pudding cake

Ingredients

- 175ml canned unsweetened coconut milk
- 0.25 tsp salt
- Toasted coconut, for garnish, optional
- 120ml limeade concentrate, thawed

- 3 large eggs at room temperature, separated
- 150g caster sugar
- 35g plain flour
- 30g unsalted butter, softened, plus extra to grease the tin

Method

1) Begin boiling the water as soon as you turn on the oven so it is ready when you put the cake in. While the lime concentrate thaws in the microwave, separate the eggs. The oven should be preheated to 160C/Gas 3 with a rack in the center. Set a 1L gratin dish or 20cm round cake pan in a roasting pan after lightly buttering it.

2) Using a hand-held electric mixer, combine the 100g of sugar and 30g of butter in a large bowl and beat until creamy. Salt, coconut milk, limeade concentrate, egg yolks, and flour should all be beaten in after the flour.

3) Thoroughly clean the beaters to ensure that no residue from this mixture is left behind for the fluffiest egg whites. The egg whites should be whipped in another medium dish until soft peaks form. Whip until stiff, glossy peaks form, then gradually add the remaining 50g of granulated sugar while still whipping. Fold in a quarter of the egg whites before adding the rest to the coconut-lime mixture.

4) Pour the batter into the dish or cake tin that has been prepared, and then fill the roasting pan with boiling water until it reaches halfway up the side of the dish or cake tin. Bake the pudding cake for 35 minutes, or until the top is brown and somewhat puffy. Remove from the water bath and let cool for 10 minutes on a wire rack.

5) Serve warm, and if preferred, top each serving with toasted coconut. Cook's Tip:

Baking the cake in a water bath will guarantee even baking and the preservation of the bottom's delicious sauce.

Yummy Brownie Muffins

Ingredients

- Fresh berries, for serving
- 1 can 100% pure pumpkin
- 1 box devil's food cake mix

Method

1) Turn the oven on to 200 C.

2) Add cake mix to a big bowl, then whisk to get rid of any lumps. Stir in the pumpkin until it is evenly distributed and fully smooth.

3) Cook's Note: Leave out any additional ingredients, such as eggs, oil, or water, that may be listed on the cake mix box. You might be tempted to add more ingredients to the mixture because it will be so thick to level out the batter. Avoid doing this!

4) Pour the batter into a 12-cup muffin tray that has been coated with non-stick spray and/or lined with foil baking cups. Bake the pan in the oven for about 20 minutes, or until a toothpick inserted into the center of a muffin comes out clean.

5) After a brief period of cooling, serve. If using, garnish with fresh berries. Enjoy!

Sour Cream Pecan Coffee Cake

Ingredients
- 1/2 unsalted butter, melted
- 1/4 tsp ground allspice
- 1/2 tsp bicarbonate of soda
- 1 1/4 cups sugar
- 1 1/2 cups sour cream
- 2 tsp vanilla extract

- 2 large eggs
- 1 tsp salt
- 1 tbsp baking powder
- 1 tsp ground cinnamon
- 1/4 cup plain flour
- 1/2 cup packed dark brown sugar
- 3 tbsp unsalted butter, melted
- 3/4 cup chopped pecans
- 2 cups plain flour

Method

1) Grease a 9-inch square pan and preheat the oven to 350°F.

2) To make the streusel, whisk together the brown sugar, flour, and cinnamon before adding the melted butter. Add the pecans and stir; then, set aside.

3) Sift the flour, baking powder, salt, baking soda, and allspice for the cake. Whisk the melted butter, sugar, sour cream, eggs, and vanilla in a separate basin. This should be

thoroughly mixed into the flour mixture. In the pan that has been prepared, distribute half of the batter, then top with half of the streusel. Stir the streusel into the batter a little using a skewer or paring knife. Spread the remaining batter on top, cover it with the remaining streusel, and give the cake one last swirl.

4) Bake the cake for 45 to 55 minutes, or until an inserted tester emerges clean. Before slicing, let the cake in the pan cool to room temperature.

5) The cake keeps for up to 3 days when properly wrapped and left out of the fridge.

Carrot Muffins

Ingredients

- 1/3 cup vegetable oil
- 2 large eggs
- 1 tablespoon pure vanilla extract
- 4 medium carrots, grated
- 1/2 cup tinned pineapple, crushed and drained

- Pinch fine salt
- 1/2 teaspoon bicarbonate of soda
- 1/2 cup wholemeal flour
- 2/3 cup dark brown sugar
- 2 teaspoons ground cinnamon
- 1 teaspoon baking powder
- 3/4 cup plain flour

Method

1) Set the oven's temperature to 350 F. Paper muffin liners should be used to line twelve and 1/2 cups of Muffin.

2) In a larger basin, combine the flour with the salt, baking powder, baking soda, wheat germ, brown sugar, and cinnamon. Egg, vegetable oil, and vanilla essence Whisked together in another medium bowl.

3) Using a rubber spatula, quickly and delicately incorporate the wet components into the dry ingredients. The batter will be extremely thick; mix in the carrots and

pineapple until they are moistened throughout. Evenly distribute the batter among the muffin tins. Bake for about 30 minutes, or until brown and a toothpick inserted in the center comes out clean. Remove muffins from tins and let them cool on a rack. Serve hot.

Chocolate Sables

Ingredients

- 50g caster sugar
- 100g light brown sugar
- 175g dark chocolate (65-70% cocoa solids) roughly chopped
- 200g unsalted butter, room temperature

- 1 1/2 tsp flaked sea salt
- 40g cocoa powder
- 3/4 tsp bicarbonate of soda
- 275g white spelt or plain flour

Method

1) In a larger basin, combine the flour, cocoa powder, baking soda, and salt; set it aside until needed.

2) In a large basin, combine the butter and sugars. Beat until smooth and creamy. Keep in mind that this isn't a cake, so the mixture doesn't need to be fluffy.

3) Add the flour mixture and stir everything together until it resembles sand with a low-speed mixer. Sable, which French means sandy, refers to this stage of baking and the final cookie's texture. The final cookie will have a little firmer texture and won't melt in your mouth if you mix the ingredients until you get a homogenous dough. Mix in the chocolate after adding it.

The mixture should be poured out onto the work area and brought together by gently kneading. Roll the dough into logs that are about 4 cm in diameter after dividing it in half. Clingfilm it up and put it in the fridge. At this stage, I usually freeze half of the dough so that I may use it to make cookies in an emergency (which happens more often than you might think!). The dough should be chilled for a few hours to firm up.

4) Set the oven's temperature to 180 degrees Celsius/160 degrees fan and line two baking trays with parchment paper. Cut the log into cookies with a thin, sharp knife that is about 1 cm thick. If the cookies break, gently press them back together. Place the prepared baking trays on top, and bake for 10 to 12 minutes, or until the mixture is spread out and just beginning to set at the edges but still appears underdone in the center. Ten minutes of cooling on the tray should be given before moving it to a wire rack to finish cooling. These cookies will stay

wonderfully fresh for a few days if they are kept in a sealed container.

Easy Apple Fritter Doughnuts

Ingredients

- 1 tsp ground cinnamon
- 1 tsp baking powder
- 1 3/4 cup plain flour
- 1/4 tsp ground nutmeg

- 1/4 tsp salt
- Icing sugar for dusting
- Vegetable oil for frying
- 2 1/2 tbsp unsalted butter, melted
- 2 large eggs, separated
- 1/2 cup plus 2 tbsp sugar
- 2 tbsp lemon juice
- 1 tsp lemon zest
- 2 medium tart apples, peeled and coarsely grated
- 3 tbsp sugar
- Pinch ground cinnamon
- 2/3 cup sour cream

Method

1) Combine the grated apple with the cinnamon, lemon zest, and lemon juice. Let the mixture sit for a few minutes to allow the apple to soften.

2) Combine the sour cream, egg yolks, and 1/2 cup of sugar in a bowl. Add the grated apple and any juices after stirring. Sift the

flour, baking powder, cinnamon, nutmeg, and salt in a separate basin. Add the melted butter after blending this into the sour cream mixture. The egg whites should be whipped until frothy before being added, along with 2 teaspoons of sugar, and continued until they hold a soft peak. Use the batter right soon after folding in the whites.

3) Following the manufacturer's instructions, pour the oil into a tabletop deep fryer (or into a sizable, deep pot so that it is only approximately 3 inches full). Use a candy thermometer if you're frying doughnuts in a pot to heat the oil to 350°F. Place a cooling rack on top of a baking sheet that has been lined with paper towels. Using a tiny ice cream scoop, carefully drop scoops of batter into the oil, leaving space between each one to allow for even cooking. Using a slotted spoon, remove the fritters after cooking them for about 3 minutes on each

side. Let them drain and cool for at least 10 minutes before dusting and serving.

4) On the day they are made, the fritters can be eaten warm or at room temperature.

Printed in Dunstable, United Kingdom